BRITAIN IN OLD PH

G000245728

AROUND THE CORNISH COAST

PETER Q. TRELOAR

Frontispiece: Postcard photographers loved to record the picturesque narrow streets of the Cornish fishing villages and the colourful characters to be found there. This is a splendid example of such work showing a street in St Ives, posted in 1908. The sails of fishing boats in the harbour can be seen in the distance, washing hangs over the street and some local inhabitants have been posed in the foreground. There even appears to be a solitary cockerel.

First published 2011

The History Press
The Mill, Brimscombe Port
Stroud, Gloucestershire, GL5 2QG
www.thehistorypress.co.uk

British Library Cataloguing in Publication Data.
A catalogue record for this book is available from the British Library.

ISBN 978 0 7524 5784 0

Typesetting and origination by The History Press
Manufacturing managed by Jellyfish Print Solutions Ltd.
Printed in India

CONTENTS

INTRODUCTION

As a Cornishman born and bred, although now living elsewhere, I have for many years enjoyed collecting old postcards of the county. I was therefore delighted when given the opportunity to make a selection from these cards to produce a picture-story of the Cornish coast

I have structured the book as though following the coastal path from Morwenstow, on the far northern boundary, down the North Coast to Land's End, around Mount's Bay to The Lizard then up the South Coast to terminate at Torpoint. Of course, no designated coastal path existed when most of the photos were taken and even today there are gaps where rivers have to be crossed. As to the rivers, although the great south coast estuaries are tidal far inland, I have not considered the inland parts to be 'coast' and so have not gone far inside the entrances.

The reader may detect some bias in my coverage. Coming from Praa Sands, I have naturally tended to acquire many cards of the Mount's Bay area and know it best. I find the old cards of the ports and harbours, with their sailing ships and fishing boats, provide a great deal more interest than shots of the coastline. Thankfully, the coast is still largely unchanged, while the harbours have been transformed totally. I have tried to give a little historical background; this also tends to relate to the settlements rather than the coast. I hope that, nonetheless, I have given reasonable coverage of the whole of the coastline, despite some unavoidable gaps.

The cards cover roughly from 1890 to 1960. At the beginning of the period, Cornwall had a very distinctive character of its own. On the coast, fishing was the predominant activity, while some tin and copper mines were still active in coastal areas. All fishing boats were sail-driven and were of distinctive local types. The great pilchard fishery, although in decline, was still important; while the seine boats were drawn up awaiting action in every major fishing location. Sail was also supreme in the coastal trades, which still handled a great deal of the county's commerce, with ketches finding their way into every creek and far up the rivers.

All this changed in the first decades of the twentieth century, as fishing declined, the pilchards disappeared and motors replaced the sail in the remaining boats. The trading ketches gradually vanished too, replaced in the larger ports by steam or motor coasters and eventually the motor lorry. After these changes, much of Cornwall's distinctive character was lost.

Developments in internal transport also made a great impact. The railway through Cornwall was completed in 1859 and became fully inter-connected with the rest of the country with the end of the broad gauge in 1892. A fairly comprehensive network was completed by the opening of the Newquay-Truro branch in 1905. The railways brought in a flood of visitors, changing the emphasis of local activity in popular destinations to tourism, and ending some of the isolation and distinctiveness of the west. They also gave a great boost to the fishing and horticultural industries. The Great Western Railway pioneered local buses, which further opened up the outlying areas and signalled the beginning of the motor age. All this has contributed to making Cornwall more like the rest of England and means that, in the summer months at least, the county is dominated by holidaymakers. But, despite all the changes, the magnificent and varied coastline, the little harbours and the glorious beaches can never lose their attraction.

Peter Q. Treloar, 2011

ACKNOWLEDGEMENTS & BIBLIOGRAPHY

My main acknowledgement must be to the photographers and publishers who produced the postcards copied in this book. Especially in earlier days when photographic equipment was heavy and clumsy and processing difficult, they did a wonderful job of recording the contemporary scene. While some took straightforward shots, many had an eye for a picture that produced artistic results. We should all be grateful to them. I would like to mention H.A.Hawke of Helston, whom I met when I was a boy. He seems to have recorded almost the whole coastline. Many of his views are, unfortunately, poorly printed and I do not know what has become of his invaluable negatives, but his cards that are left are a great resource. My thanks also to Gibsons of Scilly for permission to use some of their amazing gallery of wreck pictures.

I had thought of including a map in the book but found it hard to find a way of inserting one large enough to give useful detail. If readers wish to follow me round the coast on a map I suggest getting one of the guides to the coastal footpath produced by the National Trust and others. The Ordnance Survey 1:50,000 maps are hard to use because you need five to cover the county but a good road atlas does very well.

It is remarkable that many of my queries have been answered by a quick look at the internet, but books are still my favourite resource and among the many I have consulted are:

Carter, C., *The Port of Penzance* (Black Dwarf, 1998)

Farr, G. & Noall, C., *Wreck and Rescue Round the Cornish Coast* (Bradford Barton, 1964)

Greenhill, B., *The Merchant Schooners* (Conway Maritime Press, 1951)

Harris, H. & Ellis, M., *The Bude Canal* (David & Charles, 1972)

Harris, K., *Hevva!, Cornish Fishing in the Days of Sail* (Dyllansow Truran, 1983)

Jenkins, S.C. & Langley R.C., *The West Cornwall Railway* (Oakwood, 2002)

Kittridge, A., *Steamers and Ferries of the Tamar and Three Towns District* (Twelveheads, 2003)

Larn, R. & Carter C., *Cornish Shipwrecks, South Coast* (David & Charles, 1969)

Larn, R. & Carter, C., *Cornish Shipwrecks, North Coast* (David & Charles, 1970)

Pearce, J., *The Wesleys in Cornwall*, (Bradford Barton, 1964)

Pearse, R., *The Ports and Harbours of Cornwall*, (H.E.Warne, 1963)

Pevsner, N., *The Buildings of England Cornwall* (Penguin, 1951)

Pyatt, E.C., *Cornwall Coast Path* (HMSO, 1976)

Sagar-Fenton, M., *The Rosebud and the Newlyn Clearances* (Truran, 2003)

Vaughan J., *Rails to Newquay* (Oakwood, 2008)

1

MORWENSTOW TO NEWQUAY

The cliffs at Morwenstow epitomise the rugged, harsh atmosphere of much of the north Cornish coast, where, for shipping, the dangers are many and the refuges few.

The church of St Morwenna at Morwenstow is built above the cliffs. It has architectural elements from the Norman era onwards and a typical Cornish tower. It is renowned for its nineteenth-century vicar, 'Parson' Hawker, who befriended shipwrecked mariners and wrote Cornish-themed poetry including that near-anthem of Cornwall, 'And Shall Trelawney Die'.

There are few havens for shipping along the north coast and those that can be found are dangerous in one way or another. Bude is the first as we move south. This card shows the forbidding coastline stretching north of Bude towards Morwenstow. The old adage was: 'From Padstow Point to Harty Light, 'Tis a watery grave by day and by night.' Harty means Hartland, the most northerly point of this long north-west facing strip of the coast of Cornwall and Devon

Bude has a natural inlet, hazardous to approach in bad weather, supplemented by a canal which provides a non-tidal basin reachable through a lock. The Bude Canal was built in 1819-25 and reached as far as Crossgate near Launceston and Blagdonmoor near Holsworthy. It was unusual in having a series of inclined planes up which the boats were hauled by water weight systems. This limited the craft used to a special design of small tub-boats, four of which can be seen alongside the towpath in the card. A major function of the canal was to carry sand from the beach inland to be used as fertiliser. The tramway to carry sand up from the beach can also be seen. The canal closed at the end of the nineteenth century, leaving only the basin at Bude as its memorial.

The rocky approach to Bude has many interesting formations, notably this 'whale back' folded strata.

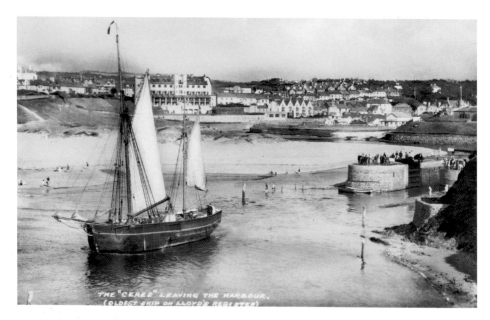

The ketch *Ceres* leaving the lock at Bude; she was a famous vessel, recorded on the card as the oldest on Lloyd's Register. She was launched at Salcombe in 1811 and is said to have taken supplies for Wellington to the Peninsular War. She was bought by Bude owners in 1852 then re-rigged in 1865 and subsequently lengthened by 15ft. She had an auxiliary engine installed in 1912 and traded until 1936 when she sprang a leak off Appledore and went down without loss of life. Apart from her longevity, she was a typical trading ketch of the Cornish coast.

South of Bude the cliffs continue grand or forbidding, according to taste, but are broken by the fine long beach of Widemouth Bay, seen here looking north towards Bude, with Black Rock prominent in its centre. Early in his career the novelist and poet Thomas Hardy visited St Juliot in pursuance of his architectural work and was entranced by the coastal scenery. Catching it in sunny and striking moods, he wrote: 'O the opal and the sapphire of that wandering western sea', and then, 'What if still in chasmal beauty looms that wild weird western shore?' (From *Beeny Cliff*, the cliff being just north of Boscastle)

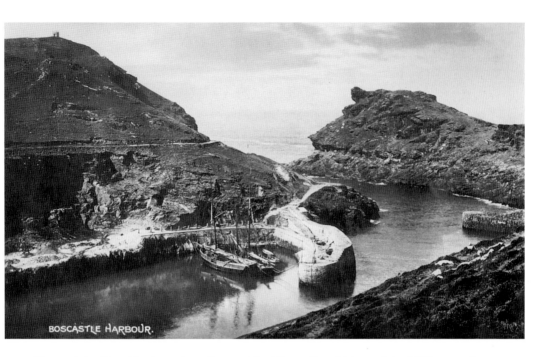

BOSCASTLE HARBOUR.

The next significant harbour down the coast is at Boscastle, which consists of little more than a narrow gorge in the cliffs. The difficult, winding entrance is shown, with three ketches, which have braved the access, moored behind the breakwater. Dating from the sixteenth century, the breakwater was built to help protect the harbour at Boscastle.

THE HARBOUR, BOSCASTLE
PHOTO. R. WEBBER

Looking inland at Boscastle you can see the diminutive harbour with the village clustering at the foot of the valley. On 16 August 2004 Boscastle was devastated by a flash flood which without warning came hurtling down the valley. Much damage was done and the harbour was filled with debris, including vehicles. Miraculously no lives were lost and most of the damage has now, laboriously, been made good.

Tintagel Castle is famous for its legendary connection with King Arthur, but that is no more than legend. There is evidence of Celtic occupation around AD 500 but the remains of the castle date from the twelfth and thirteen centuries. The site is magnificent; Tennyson described the area as 'black cliffs and caves and storm and wind'.

Below the castle is a little cove where trading vessels ventured in good weather. The derrick which lowered slate for export onto the sand can be seen at the bottom of the track zigzagging down the cliff.

A short way along the coast a narrow valley cuts through the cliffs down to Trebarwith Strand. The card shows the bottom of the valley with heavy seas breaking on the Strand and Gull Rock out in the bay.

A Spring Tide, Trebarwith Strand

A close up of the heavy waves obliterating the beach on Trebarwith Strand.

Summer Delights on Trebarwith Beach

When the tide is out and the sea calm an attractive little beach emerges at Trebarwith. Families play on the sand and in the sea while Penhallic Point looms in the background.

PORTGAVERNE

Next along are the twin coves of Port Gaverne and Port Isaac. The card, posted in 1962, shows the former with its small settlement and a few boats.

A TIGHT FIT AT PORT ISAAC.   A.6

Over the intervening headland, Lobber Point, is the larger village of Port Isaac. The card shows the unusual sight of the lifeboat being hauled up the street to its house by manpower. The card was posted in 1955 and reads, 'Having a wonderful time here in Cornwall & luckily the weather is good. Have seen a lifeboat being launched, King Arthur's Castle & have visited a china clay pit.'

The lifeboat the author saw must have been elsewhere, as the Port Isaac station was only open between 1869 and 1933, during which time eighty-six lives were saved and haulage through the street ended in the 1920s. The little cove once had a thriving pilchard fishery and exported slates from Delabole Quarry, 5 miles inland.

Padstow is near the mouth of the River Camel, which has the only significant estuary on the north coast. Unfortunately the approach from the sea involves hazarding the Doom Bar, which has seen many a shipwreck. The card, posted in 1907, shows the old harbour; the oldest parts of which date from the sixteenth century. There are at least four sizeable trading vessels, mostly topsail schooners, two white-sailed boats which may be yachts and, in the foreground, two small ketches apparently loaded with coal. Perhaps they had transhipped it from larger craft and would deliver it up-river or to coves along the coast.

Fishing Boats in Padstow Harbour

A fleet of fishing boats anchored in the estuary at Padstow, looking seawards. Like those seen later at Penzance, they have Lowestoft registration letters and so are east-coast boats working around the country, probably following the herring shoals. They are of totally different design from the Cornish luggers, with their tall main and short mizzen masts and fore-and-aft sails. Padstow is nowadays known more as a resort than a port, although it still has fishing boats which bring in supplies for the seafood restaurants for which the town is famous. Padstow is also well-known for its Hobby Horse celebration on 1 May, when the revellers sing: 'With a merry ring with the joyful spring, for summer is a-come unto day.'

Padstow's career as a resort took off when the London & South Western Railway arrived from Waterloo, after a very slow advance across north Cornwall, in 1899. This view across the inner harbour shows the hotel built to welcome the railway and LSWR trucks on the pier. John Betejman caught the mood of the train trip: 'Can it really be that this same carriage came from Waterloo? On Wadebridge station what a breath of sea scented the Camel valley!'

The same view from further back so that the Camel estuary can be seen on the left going inland towards Wadebridge. The hotel is even more prominent and the railway station and goods shed can be seen on its left. The railway subsequently extended the pier on the left to handle the increased fish traffic it generated. The railway sadly closed in 1967 and its course is now the popular Camel Trail for walkers and cyclists.

Across the Camel from Padstow are the resorts of Rock, Trebetherick and Polzeath, the area beloved of John Betjeman and exposed in the news in 2010 as the holiday choice of Prime Minister David Cameron on the occasion of the unexpectedly early birth of his daughter Endellion. The card is captioned Polzeath, but shows Hayle Bay (not to be confused with the Hayle in St Ives Bay), on the inner end of which Polzeath lies, with Pentire Point in the background.

Moving west along the coast from the Camel, we reach Trevose Head, the most prominent projection on the whole of the north coast. It fills the background in this view of the attractive beach at Mother Ivy's Bay, Harlyn.

Striking a few miles south, Porthcowan Beach lies in a sudden rectangular arm of the sea cut into the low cliffs, as seen in this aerial view.

Continuing south past Park Head we arrive at one of the best-known beauty spots on the coast: Bedruthan Steps. The series of short headlands and rocky islets, with the ever-changing tide, make for a fascinating scene, as this card looking southward shows. Legend has it that the giant Bedruthan used the rocks as stepping stones, hence the name.

Another inlet into the coast creates Mawgan Porth, seen here at low tide looking north.

Newquay's splendid beaches begin just to the south of Mawgan Porth, but this card shows the headland in Newquay's early days as a resort, when the only building visible was the new lifeboat house of 1895. The card is indistinct and rather hard to interpret. The caption refers to Lifeboat Launch but none is visible, unless one of the specks on the sea is the lifeboat. A large crowd has assembled to watch, so something must be happening. Under the two white shades are three wonderful perambulators, with small leading wheels and large rear ones. The Headland Hotel on opened at left in 1906, so this photo must have been taken before it was begun, probably when the lifeboat house was new. The Harbour and beach are hidden below the cliff.

The Sands, Newquay

An Edwardian scene at Towan Beach in Newquay. Horse-drawn mobile bathing huts are parked at the water's edge to allow discreet entry into the water. No sign of surfing!

Newquay's development as a resort began at the end of the nineteenth century, especially after the end of the Great Western Railway's broad gauge meant that the line from St Blazey, that had carried passengers since 1876, could be connected to the national system. The Atlantic Hotel is already prominent in the background.

Although the railway began Newquay's expansion, it was motorised road transport that led to its greatest growth. This card posted in 1933 illustrates the early motor age and makes an amusing contrast with the last. Gone is the paraphernalia of Edwardian beach-going, as simply-clad bathers enjoy the sea, even clutching a couple of 'body-boards', a first sign of the interest in surfing. Since then, of course, Newquay has gone on to become 'the surfing capital of England'.

The Sands from Towan Head

Looking across to the central beaches from Towan Head, showing the cliff-top lined with hotels and other development. A fairly rare visitor in the shape of a Campbells' paddle steamer lies off-shore, probably on a day trip from Ilfracombe.

The Harbour Newquay

The harbour at Newquay dates back to medieval times. It was enlarged in the early nineteenth century then was acquired in 1838 by Thomas Treffry of Fowey, a leading entrepreneur in the development of local minerals. He opened horse-worked tramways from the East Wheal Rose lead mine and St Dennis which ended at the harbour by dropping down an incline through a tunnel. The tramways were later incorporated into the Cornwall Minerals Railway and became conventional railways, but the line from station to harbour remained a horse tramway. The mouth of the tunnel can be seen towards the left while the additional central pier was built by the railway.

Looking from above the tunnel the rail layout can be seen. The tracks emerge from the tunnel at centre and serve both quays by reversing Vs. There are four trucks in the foreground, two of them loaded with coal waiting to be hauled up through the tunnel by the stationary steam engine at the top. The other two are white from the china clay they have delivered to the ships. Two shunting horses can just be made out alongside them. The nearer vessel is quite a large tri-masted topsail schooner. The tramway fell out of use in the 1920s concurrently with the death of coastal trade by sail. A footpath now follows the tramway's route through the town.

NEWQUAY, LIFEBOAT DAY, LEAVING THE SLIP.

Newquay's first lifeboat arrived in 1860 but it was not until 1895 that the station was moved to Towan Head, where a slipway was constructed that was the steepest in the country at 1 in 2¼. The spectacular launch down this slip, as seen on this card, was a popular spectacle. The station closed in 1934 by which time over 100 lives had been saved but a lifeboat was stationed in the harbour during the Second World War. Nowadays theRoyal National Lifeboat Institution (RNLI) provides inshore craft to care for the surfers and yachtsmen.

23

A survival from earlier times is the Huers' house on Towan Head. Huers were stationed on the cliffs to look out for shoals of pilchards and raise hue and cry when they were sighted, shouting 'Heva, heva' and directing the waiting pilchard fishery boats to the fish. Although huers operated all round the Cornish coast, this provision for their comfort is a unique survivor.

Last of the great Newquay beaches is Fistral Bay, round to the south of Towan Head, seen in the background on this card. The sweeping rollers and sandy beach explain its attraction to surfers.

2

PERRANPORTH
TO ST IVES

ARCH & ROCKS, PERRANPORTH

The next major beach southward along the coast is Perran. Where the cliffs retreat behind sand dunes, the resort of Perranporth developed in the early years of the twentieth century, helped by the opening of the Newquay-St Agnes-Truro branch railway in 1905. There are also impressively-shaped cliffs as shown on this postcard.

St Agnes is a little way inland, its nearest point on the coast being Trevaunance Cove. The valley, cove and tall cliffs running north beyond it are all shown on this card.

A closer view of the bottom of the valley at Trevaunance showing tin-streaming works and the little harbour constructed under the cliff. In the days when St Agnes was a great tin mining district and for years afterwards, it paid to stream the water flowing from the mining area to extract the metal which had escaped from the processes at the mines.

The harbour at Trevaunance was a remarkable phenomenon. Beginning in the early eighteenth century it was built, or partially so, five times and every time, in its exposed position under the cliff, it was destroyed and swept away by the sea. The aim was to provide a north coast port for Truro and to serve the St Agnes mining district. The final attempt began in 1793 and produced the harbour seen here.

This card, posted in 1911 (but probably produced earlier) shows two ketches in the harbour, one drying its sails. The immense solidity of the breakwater can be seen. So can the old wooden staging and apparatus for loading vessels from the heights and the precipitous stairway or ladder leading from staging to harbour.

A final look at Trevaunance on this card posted in 1929. There is now a holidaymakers' beach in the foreground but the harbour, having fallen into disuse, has almost been destroyed by the sea, despite its solidity. The staging has gone and only the steep steps seem to survive.

A few miles down the coast, Porthtowan was also once close to much mining activity and so tin steamers set up business on the beach. This rather faded card, posted in 1904, shows their launders and troughs. The buildings in the background seem to belong to the burgeoning holiday business.

Portreath Looking Seaward.

The harbour at Portreath was an entirely artificial one, created by cutting a channel under the cliff on the north side of a sandy bay. It was made in the late eighteenth century. In 1810 the Poldice Tramway connected it with the rich copper-mining area north of Redruth.

By the mid-nineteenth century, the little makeshift port had to handle the greater part of the enormous sea-borne trade of this amazing conglomeration of metalliferous mines. On the card there are three steamers in the harbour, huge heaps of coal and at least two railway trucks.

Looking south over Portreath beach with the entrance to the harbour in the foreground.
Entry in heavy weather was very hazardous.

Cable Railway, Portreath

Argall s Series

As well as the Poldice Tramway, Portreath was served by a branch of the early Hayle Railway,
opened in 1837. It terminated in this long incline down from the plateau to the harbour,
which was worked by a stationary steam engine at the top. Two trucks can be seen at the
bottom of the incline just outside the harbour precincts. The incline ceased to be used in
1930; by then the port was in sharp decline. The harbour has now been built around with
residential development, but only pleasure craft use it.

Hayle Beach.

Hayle, From Lelant Ferry.

This postcard of Hayle from The Towans was posted in 1909. It shows Hayle as a thriving port and industrial centre. There are at least three steamers and a number of large sailing ships in the harbour. Harveys' famous foundry is on the right in the distance. It produced everything from great steam pumping engines for the mines to steamships, but due to the closure of the mines, it was already in decline by the time of the picture. Hayle also housed copper smelting works in earlier years and later again but on the side of the river in the foreground, there was a First World War explosives factory, which became a chemical works, and an electricity generating station.

All industrial activity has now ceased and the harbour is very quiet. The viaduct crossing the town in the distance carries the main railway line from Truro to Penzance. It was built as a timber structure by the West Cornwall Railway in 1852 and rebuilt with masonry piers and iron girders in 1886, in which form it has lasted, with repairs, to the present day. A branch railway ran from the north end of the viaduct down to the docks where railway trucks can be seen in the foreground, behind the traction engine.

Opposite above: Passing more rugged cliffs with such chilling names as Deadman's Cove and Hell's Mouth and rounding Godrevy Point, we reach Gwithian and Hayle Towans. Sand dunes mark the end of the great cliffs which we have followed all down the north Cornish coast. There is a good beach edging the dunes, seen here well populated with children, while beyond, the Penwith Peninsula prorudes behind the entrance to Hayle harbour.

Opposite below: The harbour mouth at Hayle, with the shed and boats of Lelant Ferry in the foreground. The Ferry was an ancient one. Its use considerably shortened the journey from Penwith to the north, cutting out a long detour via St Erth in the days before the causeway from Hayle to St Erth was built. Even after the causeway was built, the ferry continued to operate regularly until 1962 with a brief revival thereafter. There appears to have been a somewhat risky ford at low tide at the same location. The spit in the middle of the picture divides the shallow tidal lake of Lelant Saltings on the right from Hayle Harbour on the left.

A remarkable postcard used in 1908 which helpfully explains that these are the St Ives fishing boats, laid up for the winter; the location being Lelant Saltings. Various types of lugger can be made out (mostly the local pointed-stern type), the forest of masts extending as far as the eye can see. It was probably only the smaller pilchard drivers which were laid up in this way.

The coast of Penwith runs north-west from Lelant to St Ives past Carbis Bay, where a small resort has developed above the beach. The branch railway from St Erth to St Ives cuts through the headlands on each side and runs round above the bay, as can be seen. The station is towards top right.

A view of St Ives, looking from the west over the town to the harbour and The Island. The settlement developed gradually from the early Middle Ages and by the eighteenth century was a significant fishing and trading port. Its picturesque harbour and fine location made it an obvious target for the developing tourist trade in the late nineteenth and twentieth centuries. More recently it has found fame as an artists' colony, crowned by the opening of Tate St Ives in 1993.

An early card of Porthminster Beach, the harbour and the The Island. Drawn up above the beach are the seine boats of the pilchard fishery, awaiting the arrival of the shoals.

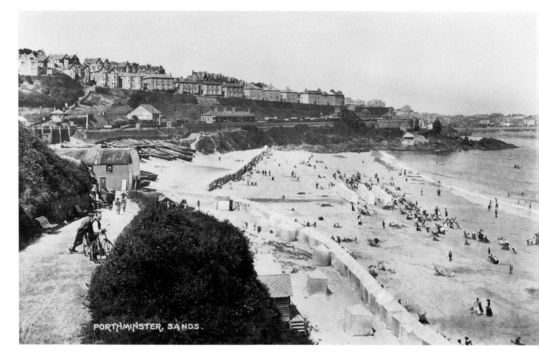

PORTHMINSTER, SANDS.

By way of contrast, Porthminster at a later date. The beach is crowded with bathing tents but the seine boats are still there, probably disused. Above the beach is the railway station. The branch from St Erth opened in 1877 and continues to serve, boosted by park-and-ride traffic from Lelant Saltings, but the station seen here has gone, replaced by a car park and a single dead-end line.

A very early undivided back postcard, posted to France in 1903, which shows the harbour packed with fishing luggers. There were some 200 registered in the port in 1905. The breakwater was designed by Thomas Smeaton to replace an earlier one and was completed in 1770.

"*A peaceful harbour.*"

A study of fishing luggers at St Ives, sentimentally captioned 'A peaceful harbour'. All those visible have two masts and many have hoisted their tan sails to dry them. The smaller boats, known as pilchard drivers, were used in coastal waters but the larger mackerel drivers made long voyages far from home, sailing regularly to follow the herring to the Irish and North Seas. For speed and seaworthiness the luggers of west Cornwall were without peer.

THE HARBOUR ST IVES.

Another record of shipping in the harbour, this card was posted in 1912. In addition to the luggers on the left, there is an assembly of five trading ketches either awaiting cargoes (probably salted fish) or escaping bad weather. The tower of the fifteenth-century church of St Ia is on the right.

35

A fishing boat of later days makes good speed out of St Ives. She is SS95 *Sweet Promise* and has the lines, including pointed stern, of a local mackerel driver, so is possibly a sailing lugger reconstructed with an engine. The coast behind leads away to Carbis Bay and Hayle.

Fish sales at St Ives were a popular subject for cards. This scene at the top of the harbour shows that fish were carried in boxes between long poles as well as baskets.

A more modern fish sale, remarkable for the size of the fish laid out on the sand. Transport away from the harbour was still by horse and cart.

St Ives became a lifeboat station in 1840. The boat is stationed at the harbour-side and hauled to the sea by tractor if necessary. The card shows a rowing lifeboat in the harbour. The station suffered disastrous loss of its boats in 1938 and 1939 but continues to this day, the Lifeboat House being a great attraction to visitors.

Seining for pilchards off Porthminster beach. The seine boats have surrounded a shoal with nets and are preparing to haul in the catch. Pilchard fishing was a huge industry all around the Cornish coast in the nineteenth century but declined in the first two decades of the twentieth. The shoals arrived near the coast in July; harvest time, hence the rhyme, 'When the corn is in the shock, then the fish are on the rock.' Guided by the Huer, the seine boats (owned by co-operatives known as companies) surrounded the shoals with nets and then 'tucked' them into the boats and got them ashore. It is recorded that in 1851 a single shoal at St Ives produced over 16 million fish.

A last look at St Ives on an atmospheric card, posted in 1952, entitled 'Gossip'. Behind the group there is a then more modern type of motor fishing boat with wheelhouse but the small steam drifter PZ277 on the left is from an earlier age and unusual for the area.

3

PENWITH: CLODGY
POINT TO MOUSEHOLE

Clodgy Points, St Ives.

From St Ives the coastline turns south towards Lands End at Clodgy Point. I have seen this view described as 'Five Points' but my map identifies only Clodgy, Hor, Pen Enys and Carn Naun Points. Perhaps the first projection is too insignificant to be named on a map. Anyway, the Edwardian lady and her daughter seem to be taking them all in.

On the coast road from St Ives to St Just, Zennor is a little village in an exposed position on the top of the cliffs. It is built of the local granite and surrounded by granite hedges and boulders. The church of St Senara is medieval, part going back to Norman times.

Gurnard's Head is one of the many striking features along this coastline, taking its name from its supposed resemblance to a local variety of fish. There are the remains of an Iron Age fort on the promontory.

Pendeen Watch is a lookout point further along the coast from which this sight could be seen on 17 August 1919. The Italian steamship *Chimu* had struck the Brisons to the south then run aground in sinking condition off Pendeen. The photograph gives a feeling of the vastness and power of the Atlantic Ocean as it pummels the doomed vessel. (Photo courtesy of Gibsons of Scilly)

There is a rich tin and copper mining area around St Just. The minerals run out under the sea so mines were built on the cliffs to exploit them. This is Botallack, perhaps the best-known of all Cornish mines. It was productive from the late eighteenth century until the early twentieth century. In 1865 it was visited by the Duke and Duchess of Cornwall (later King Edward VII and Queen Alexandra), who went down a shaft under the sea. Afterwards the Duchess did not feel well. The tall buildings housed steam pumping and winding engines.

Just along the coast was Levant Mine. It became infamous for the accident in 1919 when the last working man-engine in Cornwall broke away from its top joint and fell down the shaft, killing thirty-one men. A man-engine was a rod moved up and down the shaft by the engine, with steps at intervals which miners had to step on and off to progress up or down. Levant survived the accident and its remains now house one of the finest relics of the Cornish mining industry. In the white building (right of centre), a steam Cornish beam winding engine survived to be rescued by the Trevithick Society. The whole site is now managed by the National Trust and the engine is regularly steamed.

Cape Cornwall with The Brisons beyond is the only headland in England with a 'Cape' name. There was a mine on its far side with a flue from the boiler house to the chimney on the summit. The chimney made too fierce a draught and was abandoned and the mine ceased production around 1870.

Natural Arch and The Brisons, St. Just

A little further south at Progo is this natural rock arch on the sand, with another view of The Brisons in the distance.

Whitesand Bay, a fine beach, leads around to Sennen Cove, seen on an early postcard, posted probably in 1904. It bears only the rather stark message, 'This is Sennen Cove. The striped shanty is the Western Union station.' Despite its exposed position, Sennen had a small fishing industry and manned a lifeboat from 1853 which carried out some heroic rescues. The station has just opened a new slipway and acquired a new lifeboat and also operates an inshore rescue craft.

I am not sure where this picture was taken, but it could perhaps be off Sennen and serves well to illustrate pilchard fishing. The men are 'tucking the seine'– that is extracting the huge shoal of trapped pilchards from the encircling net. The boat on the left seems to be a fishing lugger with mast and rigging rather than a regular seine boat like those on the right.

This card identifies Sennen as the location. The seine boat has come ashore and is being unloaded with shovel and baskets while horses and carts wait to take away the harvest of the sea. The catch was first stacked with salt and the valuable oil extracted. It was then usually packed in barrels for export, the Catholic countries of Europe being prime targets, with their need for fish on Fridays and during Lent.

High granite cliffs lead on to Land's End, seen here rather unusually from the north looking past it to the rock Enys Dodnan and Pardenack Point, this stretch of coast running in a south-easterly direction.

Looking back towards Land's End from the opposite direction on a rough day. Enys Dodnan is in the foreground, The Armed Knight beyond, while further out is the Longships reef with its lighthouse. The first lighthouse was built on the rocks in 1795 and replaced by the present one in 1873. Like all offshore lighthouses it is now unmanned and serviced via a helipad built over the lantern.

A peaceful view from the headland with the sun sparkling on a calm sea. Wesley's Stones are in the foreground and the Longships beyond. Land's End gets its name because it is the most south-westerly point of the British mainland and the most westerly point in England (work that out!). John and Charles Wesley's journals record visits to Land's End over forty years: 'We went afterwards down, as far as we could go safely towards the point of the rocks at the Land's End. It was an awful sight.' Years later they visited again and recorded ,'I know no natural curiosity like this. The vast ragged stones rise on every side when you are near the point of the land, with green turf between, as level and smooth as if it were the effect of art.' This must surely be a description of Wesley's Stones, from which John is reputed to have preached.

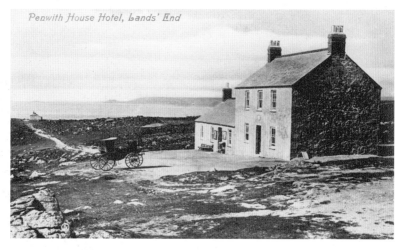

A view of the area above the headland around one hundred years ago. It makes a striking contrast with the present theme park, with only the modest Penwith House Hotel and, in the distance, the famous First and Last House. Cape Cornwall is on the horizon and a four-wheeled horse carriage waits outside the hotel to take its passengers back to Penzance.

A fine square-rigged ship, technically a four-masted barque, caught off Land's End by a Penzance photographer. She is riding high in ballast and makes a magnificent sight with all her sails set.

In sad contrast the steam collier *Llandaff* has run aground in Nanjizal Bay, just south of Land's End. She went aground in fog in 1889 and was refloated. Regrettably, she was wrecked ten years later on Bude breakwater. (Photo courtesy of Gibsons of Scilly)

The coast runs south-east to Gwennap Head then turns east and north into Mount's Bay. There are a number of rocky coves in the granite cliffs. Porthgwarra is a tiny fishing community with a rough slipway and caves in the cliffs.

The Minack Theatre occupies a magnificent position in a natural amphitheatre in the cliff near Porthcurno. There is a superb view out over the sea and across to Trewyn Dinas, in the distance here. For atmosphere, a fine night with the moon reflecting on the ocean cannot be beaten. The theatre was created by Rowena Cade, beginning with a production of *The Tempest* in 1932. The seating, props and backstage facilities have gradually been improved. This photo of a production of *King Lear* was taken some years ago, since then the once-modest permanent features have been added to; perhaps there is a danger of overdoing them. The theatre is now run by a charitable trust and usually mounts seventeen productions, by players from all over the country, every summer.

A view from the air with Trewyn Dinas to the fore. Porthcurno's shell-sand beaches are beyond and the cliffs which hide the Minack beyond them again. From 1870 Porthcurno became the starting point of numerous sub-oceanic telegraph cables; Cable and Wireless long had a major presence there, now commemorated in a museum in the valley.

On Trewyn Dinas is the Logan Rock, Logan meaning 'rocking'. Weighing some 80 tons, it has been left by erosion over eons balanced so precisely on a solid formation that it can be rocked by a single person, perhaps what the man in this photo is purporting to do. Back in 1824 a Lieutenant Goldsmith of the Royal Navy and his men, for a lark, dislodged the Rock and threw it down. Such was the outcry that the Navy required him to replace it, which he managed to do with a large workforce, massive wooden structures and expenditure of the large sum of £130 over seven months. It is said it never rocked as easily as before but it remains a popular tourist destination.

Then comes Penberth, another of the rocky little coves, again with its rough slipway and handful of boats for the inshore fishery. The card, posted in 1927, says, 'We are staying here tonight in a most gorgeous house. This a most beautiful little cove, with only a very few cottages. The coast scenery around here is very grand ...'

Just along the coast from Penberth is St Loy Bay where a strange coincidence occurred in 1912. On the night of 13 February the SS *South America*, 4197 tons, drove ashore in fog. She could not be got off and scrapping began. Then on 14 October the SS *Abertay*, 599 tons, also groping through fog, bumped in right alongside the bigger ship. She also was scrapped on site. This rather faint old postcard records the remarkable scene. (Photo courtesy of Gibsons of Scilly)

Mousehole is one of the most attractive of the small Cornish fishing ports as this photo of its small harbour and clustering village, seen from the south, shows.

Mousehole harbour full of fishing luggers in the early twentieth century. There were over 400 fishermen based in the port in the previous century. One can make out the difference between the pilchard and mackerel drivers by their size, the ones used for catching pilchards being smaller.

A close-up of the crowded luggers on a card posted in 1907. Mousehole (locally pronounced Mows'll and speculatively a corruption of the Cornish maes-hohl – hollow of the gulls) was an active fishing port in the thirteenth century. It gained its first breakwater in the fourteenth century, while the present ones came in the nineteenth century. The central lugger here is of typical Mount's Bay type with a pointed stern.

A much later view looking south over the harbour, showing motorised fishing boats with wheelhouses but also a fine three-masted schooner alongside.

The Great Western Railway produced this postcard of Mousehole in the railway's extensive pre-First World War series. It shows a good selection of large and small luggers filling the harbour at low tide. The Cornish Maritime Trust has restored a St Ives lugger, *Barnabas*, which is based at Mousehole.

A nice study of later-style fishing boats at rest in the harbour at Mousehole. The narrow entrance is at the end of pier on left. It was closed by wooden baulks in stormy weather. The larger boats would have gone far out to sea, the smaller ones would have worked inshore, probably crabbing. There is very little fishing from Mousehole these days, it is now concentrated on Newlyn.

Wesley's Pulpit Rock, Mousehole.

Left: Looking out to sea at Mousehole, the rock known as Wesley's Pulpit is in the foreground. As at Land's End, John Wesley is credited with having preached on this convenient natural pulpit. Behind, a fleet of fishing luggers is sailing by and The Lizard is on the horizon, marking the eastern limit of Mount's Bay.

Below: A final atmospheric glimpse of Mousehole on a cloudy day, showing some later fishing boats at low tide; old houses ring the harbour. Mousehole's great annual event is the display of the Christmas lights in the harbour and on the hillside, culminating in the celebrations on Tom Bocock's Eve, 23 December, when thousands come from near and far to enjoy the lights and join in carol singing, led by the Mousehole Male Voice Choir, on the harbour-side.

4

AROUND PENZANCE: NEWLYN TO ST MICHAEL'S MOUNT

PENZANCE. FROM NEWLYN.

The view looking north-east above Newlyn, with the harbour below and Penzance across the bay. Probably a 1920s view, although most of the fishing boats in the centre appear to be sail-powered. They may be French or other visitors. The big piers were built in the second half of the nineteenth century to create the present large harbour. The south pier, with lighthouse, was used for many years to ship out large quantities of roadstone from the Penlee quarry which lay just to the right.

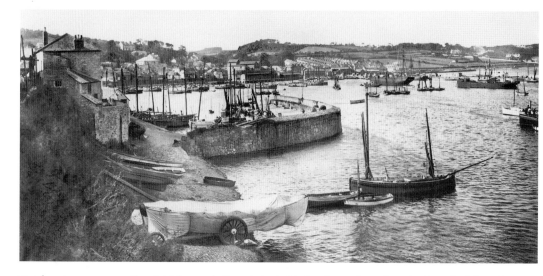

Newlyn, too, was a medieval fishing port; the original old pier shown here dates back to the fifteenth century. In the nineteenth century it was active in the mackerel, pilchard and herring fisheries. In the foreground here a typical lugger lies moored; onshore is a rowing lifeboat on wheels, carefully covered. Penzance had a lifeboat from as early as 1803 but it was relocated to Newlyn 1908-13, when this picture must have been taken of the boat *Elizabeth and Blanche*. A further move to Penlee House and slip came in 1913. After the tragic disaster of 1981, a new boat was permanently moved to Newlyn where it remains afloat at all times.

Nothing could be more representative of old Newlyn than this picture of a fish jouster, a lady selling pilchards around the district from her donkey cart. The card was posted in Penzance in 1904 to an address in Scilly: 'Dear Nan, here for two days in Mousehole, is my shoes done yet Lil'.

A classic shot of the Newlyn fishing fleet putting to sea in the days of unassisted sail.

A wooden, motorised, fishing boat of the later-type in Newlyn harbour with the village rising up the hill beyond.

At one time it was common for French sailing fishing boats from Brittany to come into Newlyn. This card, which was posted probably in the 1940s, shows a small fleet of them tied up in the harbour. I can remember seeing them sailing in about then, with their single masts and large main sail with boom and gaff. They were quite different from the Cornish boats of old.

An early card looking outward from the inner end of the harbour; two luggers rest on the bottom in the foreground. The scenery, clear light and characterful people led to the development of the Newlyn school of painters in the years before and after 1900. Their highly-prized pictures immortalised the looks and lives of the contemporary fishing community. A fine selection can be seen in the Penlee House Gallery at Penzance.

Newlyn had a warren of picturesque old streets around the inner end of the harbour in Street-an-Nowan and above the old pier in Newlyn Town. In 1936 they were threatened with clearance as slums by Penzance Borough Council, which acted with remarkable arrogance and insensitivity. This led to the famous protest during which, amid great publicity, the fishing boat *Rosebud* sailed round to Westminster with a petition against the proposals and her crew met the Minister for health. In the event some of the old houses were saved but great harm was done to the character of the village and to the community. This card of Primrose Court gives a good impression of the old Newlyn, complete with posing residents and washing hanging out to dry.

Unloading Mackerel at Newlyn

The business of Newlyn was and is fish. In this early twentieth-century scene the primitive arrangements for landing fish at the inner end of the harbour can be seen.

The Fish Market, Penzance.

More sophisticated provision was made later. Here fish are laid out for sale in a covered market alongside the road at the top of Newlyn harbour. Newlyn is now England's largest fishing port with comprehensive modern facilities.

'Fleets of Peace and War in Mount's Bay', proclaims the caption on this card. It shows the gathering of the Royal Navy's Grand Fleet outside Newlyn in 1904 just before the dreadnought-type battleships were introduced. On the peaceful side there are a sprinkling of fishing luggers, a three-masted barquentine at the main pier, a stone boat loading at the south pier and another awaiting its turn off the entrance.

A PORTION OF THE BRITISH ARMADA OF 195 WARSHIPS ASSEMBLED IN MOUNTS BAY. JULY 1910.

This photo shows 'A portion of the British Armada of 195 warships assembled in Mount's Bay, July 1910.' The card was posted on 25 July and read, 'This is just a wee bit of the Fleet. It's a great disappointment they had to leave last night on account of the gale and the King of course is not coming now. It was a proud sight seeing them in the bay.' Yes, indeed. A greater gathering of ironclads may never have taken place. The huge assembly comprised the Atlantic, Home and Mediterranean Fleets and had gathered in Mount's Bay to be reviewed by King George V, who had acceded to the throne that May. Unfortunately bad weather made it necessary for the fleet to move before the King arrived and the review took place instead at Torbay on 25 July. It is reported that the fleet at Torbay included thirty-six battleships, twenty-nine cruisers and forty-eight destroyers plus auxiliaries. The fleet off Penzance included some of the first dreadnoughts; in the first ever flight in Cornwall, Claude Grahame-White flew over the fleet on 23 July, in his Farman aircraft.

A view of Penzance from above Newlyn; probably early twentieth century. The tide is out, exposing the rocky foreshore. A strip of fields above the beach separates Penzance from Newlyn, where public gardens, subject to attack by the sea, now exist.

The Beach, Penzance.

The Promenade at Penzance seen from the beach at low tide with plenty of rocks and seaweed to engage the visitors and a scattering of small boats, which must have been removed when the sea was rough. Being pebbly and restricted, it was and is not a good beach for basking or bathing. The Promenade was an early gesture towards the tourist business by Penzance Borough, being built in 1844.

A view looking east along the Promenade on a card posted in 1907. There is a display of Edwardian attire for adults and children, while the full tide demonstrates one of the disadvantages of the beach – it is covered at high tide. The nearest three-storey building was soon to be replaced by a more grandiose structure.

At the east end of the Promenade there was once an old gun battery to defend the port. In 1935 there appeared in its place the Jubilee Pool, a fine lido in contemporary style, which commemorated the silver jubilee of King George V. The pool re-opened after renovation in 1994 and continues to provide an attractive facility for the town. The card clearly illustrates some major event, perhaps the opening or a swimming gala.

Penzance was a small port from medieval times but the modern harbour was created in the nineteenth century. The outer pier, extended in 1852 and with its iron lighthouse by Copperhouse Foundry of Hayle, serves as the mooring point for the steamers for the Isles of Scilly. This card, posted in 1907, shows an animated scene as a Scilly steamer is unloaded. Baskets, barrels and boxes must have carried vegetables, flowers and fish while a heap of empty baskets at the right awaits transport to the islands.

Penzance.

The Harbour.

This early card shows an interesting scene at the entrance to Penzance harbour. The two large fishing boats have LT registration, which means that in search of their hauls they have sailed all the way from Lowestoft. With their large hulls and gaff-rigged sails they are quite different from the local boats. Visits by east-coast boats to Mount's Bay were a feature of the fishing industry at the time. The steamer at the outer pier is small but has an even smaller steamer or launch moored alongside it. The former appears to be the *Lady of the Isles*, the first steamer specifically built for the Scilly service, by Harveys of Hayle in 1875, of only 152 tons. She served until wrecked at Lamorna in 1904 but was raised and continued another career in salvage until sunk by a mine in 1940.

More modern provision for the Scilly service. Moored at the outer pier is the *Scillonian*, the second of three vessels of that name with which the Isles of Scilly Steamship Company has successively maintained the service since 1926. The first was a steamer of 429 tons by Ailsa Shipbuilding Co. of Troon. This, the second, replaced it in 1954 and was a motor ship of 920 tons by Thorneycroft of Southampton and in turn gave way to the current *Scillonian* of 1255 tons, which was built by Appledore Shipbuilders in 1977.

The outer harbour at Penzance, in the day of the sail. The inner, floating harbour is behind the pier on the left, it was created in 1884. The dry dock is to the right behind the end of the viaduct. Penzance was late to be made a parish in its own right (it was part of Madron) and St Mary's Church on the skyline dates from 1832-5.

Penzance Harbour and Docks

A steamroller is about to cross the Ross swing bridge, which, with its approach viaduct, was opened in 1881 to create the first road round the inside of the harbour. The Bridge opens into the little-used Abbey turning pool and thus to the dry dock at right. The big white full-rigged ship is the French *Leon Bureau*, which attracted a lot of interest when it was towed into Penzance in 1909 after some mishap I have not seen explained.

The tide is high and a steamer, the *Stainburn*, has come through the swing bridge and is being manoeuvred into the dry dock for attention. She had hit the Runnelstone and caught fire in February 1906 before being towed in. A 440 ton ship of that name, presumably this one, was sunk by a U-boat on 29 October 1916 while on passage from Swansea to Honfleur. The dry dock had been enlarged in the 1880s and was run by Holmans 1904-95, during which time many damaged ships were repaired, numerous coasters and tankers and the 'Scillonians' were overhauled and several lightships were converted to automatic operation. Another company continues to run it.

The outer harbour was used for regattas and galas. Nothing is recorded of this event but it is clearly junketing of some kind. There are many spectators on Albert Pier (constructed 1845) and several small boats to the left of the flag-bedecked fishing boat. Someone is swimming alongside that boat but he does not seem to be the centre of attention. Albert Pier has a trading ketch moored to it, also full of spectators, and the Pier is piled with coal.

No depiction of Cornwall would be complete without a seagull study. This card is captioned 'Seagulls, Penzance', but on close inspection the boat is registered in St Ives and the background looks like that too. The men are working at a table covered with fish, probably preparing them as bait – no wonder the seagulls are excited.

The main-line railway cuts right through Cornwall without running alongside the coast anywhere until its final stretch along Mount's Bay to Penzance, starting from where Marazion station used to be. The West Cornwall Railway opened into Penzance in 1852 and approached the terminus across a wooden viaduct over the beach. The viaduct was many times damaged or destroyed by storms but was in good order when this photo was taken in about 1906. It shows a local train running towards the station, with the Mount visible beyond. The engine is a Great Western Railway 'Bulldog' class, quite probably and appropriately number 3340 *Marazion*. The GWR replaced the viaduct with a solid embankment in 1921.

A very atmospheric photo of the Eastern Green Beach at Penzance, seen from Marazion against a stormy evening sky. A number of silhouetted seaweed carts can just be made out.

St Michael's Mount is probably more often illustrated as a symbol of Cornwall than any other location. It fills the background of this picture, taken at low tide with two horses pulling a cartload of seaweed for use as fertiliser towards the camera. The lighter cart behind may have come over from the Mount.

At high tide the Mount becomes a true island, accessible only by boats such as those shown here at the Marazion landing. The Mount has a long history with a monastic presence from Anglo-Saxon times until the Dissolution in the sixteenth century. Since then it has served as an aristocratic residence, from about 1660 for the St Aubyn family. The summit buildings contain traces of the monastery, with accretions in almost every century since, the whole making a fine spectacle on its pinnacle and well worth a visit.

Another view of the Mount at high tide with Marazion in the foreground. In an intriguing echo of 1910, the Bay behind is full of great warships. This must have been soon after the Second World War before the Navy was run down. There are a 'King George V' class battleship at right, three fleet aircraft carriers, two cruisers and many other unidentified vessels; quite a sight! I remember the four surviving battleships of this class visiting the bay during navy days in my boyhood. They were all scrapped in 1957-8.

The Mount, seen at low tide with the causeway visible and a the dead-calm sea. In sad contrast with the last picture, the remains of the old battleship *Warspite* can be seen being gradually dismantled. The hulk had been towed round from Prussia Cove in August 1950 after it went aground there on 21 April 1947. The process of dismantling some 30,000 tons of metal was very slow and continued until 1956, the scrap being landed on the Albert Pier at Penzance.

5

EASTERN MOUNT'S BAY: PERRANUTHNOE TO GUNWALLOE

East of Marazion, the little village of Perranuthnoe has, as can be seen, a church and this small beach.

Looking eastward from Perranuthnoe beach, the view takes in Cudden Point, which ends the vista along the coast from Penzance, as beyond it the coastline falls back for some miles before projecting again towards The Lizard.

On the far side of Cudden Point is Prussia Cove, famous for its legendary connection with smugglers, one of whom, John Carter, assumed the name of 'King of Prussia' after the celebrated Frederick the Great of that country. As a result, what was Porthleah became known as Prussia Cove. It is now a very modest cove with room for a few small boats in an exposed creek.

A nice study of lobster pots and an old thatched fisherman's hut at Prussia Cove. As in many fishing coves, the people of Prussia Cove made their own pots from locally-grown withies. The roof of the hut is anchored down with ropes to save it from the wind.

HMS *Warspite* was one of the most celebrated of British battleships. Launched in 1913 she took part in the Battle of Jutland and after modernisation in the thirties had an extremely active Second World War, fighting at Narvik and in the Mediterranean (including the Battle of Matapan) and shelling over the beaches on D-Day. She was sold for scrap in 1947 and, with her guns removed, was on tow from Portsmouth to Faslane when she broke free in a gale in Mount's Bay and eventually blew ashore off Prussia Cove on 23 April 1947. I saw her come ashore: the seas were enormous; a memorable occasion. Her crew were taken off in a courageous rescue by the Penlee Lifeboat, the waves lifting the lifeboat 20ft up and down alongside the great flank of the warship. With plenty of valuable steel in her she was worth salvaging and a salvage company eventually managed to make her sufficiently buoyant to float her off, but they could not tow her further than Marazion.

Looking westward from Hoe Point in conditions very different from the 'Warspite' gale, Cudden Point, with its distinctive Coastguard house, is beyond Prussia Cove with the fine grey sand of Kenneggy Beach in the bay.

The beach at Praa Sands, looking east at half tide. Seen in the first quarter of the twentieth century before much development had taken place and a house was built on Rinsey Head in the distance. Initial growth of the private Sea Meads Estate can be seen at left and Rinsey village is on the skyline.

Praa Sands at a later date and in more summery conditions. There is a café on the left; housing has appeared on the hillside as has the house on Rinsey Head. In earlier days the area had a reputation for 'wrecking', not luring ships ashore (after all, Cornishmen constantly risked their lives to rescue those in peril on the sea), but stripping any ship providence chose to throw up on their shore. There is a, perhaps apocryphal, rhyme: 'God keep us from rocks and shelving sands and save us from Breage and Germoe mens' hands', which two parishes include the coast hereabouts.

The "Noisiel", Wrecked at Praa Sands on Aug 4th '05
Real Photo.
A.H.Hawke, Photo', Helston

In a wreck clearly the work of providence, the French barquentine *Noisiel* was blown ashore in the middle of Praa beach on 4 August 1905. She was loaded with valuable steel from a scrapped battleship. She became a total wreck and as late as the Second World War the precious steel was being recovered by blasting operations. Traces of the ship still appear in low sand conditions.

Praa Sands village seen from above Pengersick, which lies on the lane down from the main road. Hoe Point marks the western end of the beach and in the trees can be seen the Tudor period remains of Pengersick Castle. It had a tempestuous history, its lords commonly involved in smuggling and disorder.

The eastern end of Praa beach with the rocks and sands of Lesceave Por below. There is good swimming off the rocks in the right conditions. One can also see Rinsey Head, before it acquired its house, beyond.

In 1921 the steamship *Janakis*, in ballast and unmanageable in a heavy gale, blew ashore on the eastern end of Praa Sands. The picture shows that she was very fortunate to miss the rocks at the beach-end by a few yards and to stick on an unusually high ridge of sand. (Photo courtesy of Gibsons of Scilly)

Marvellous to relate, the *Janakis* was eventually refloated. This picture shows that the topography of the beach has altered completely. The ship may already have been shifted a little down to the west and a number of men are working on the sand below her. The line of stones must mark a clearance operation. The Western Marine Salvage Co. with their ships *Lady of the Isles* (*see* p.64) and *Greencastle* managed to haul her off in November 1921 and take her to Penzance for repair. The black spot in the middle of the beach marks the remnants of the less lucky *Noisiel*. (Photo courtesy of Gibsons of Scilly)

Moving on from Praa Sands on a fine summer evening with the tide right out to reveal the 'mile long golden sands' and the sun shining on the sea around Hoe and Cudden Points, with the Penwith peninsula on the horizon.

The other side of Rinsey Head lies the Cove (properly Porthcew), overlooked by its sentinel mine engine house and reached by a steep path down the cliff. Beyond is Trewarvas Point, hiding its old mine houses while The Lizard is on the skyline. The beach is of fine grey sand and is a good sheltered spot on a windy day, although the sea comes right up to the cliffs at high spring tide.

Rinsey Head, Praa Sands.

Looking the other way at Rinsey Cove, with the house on the head (a creation of the 1920s). Cudden Point can be seen above it. Interestingly, the sand at adjoining beaches along the coast, Kenneggy, Praa and Rinsey is successively grey, golden and grey and although huge quantities of sand disappear out to sea in winter, it always comes back in the same place.

Perhaps the best month to walk the Cornish cliffs is May, when flowers are at their loveliest and the clumps of thrift, in particular, make a wonderful show, as can be seen here on the high cliffs and a typical granite stone hedge at Rinsey. Betejman again captures the essence: 'The seagulls plane and circle out of sight below this thirsty, thrift-encrusted height; the veined sea-campion buds burst into white.'

Porthleven has an artificial harbour which was created where a long, low valley meets the sea. The harbour was built 1811-8 in the hope of providing a refuge for shipping on a hostile coast, but it proved too dangerous to enter in rough weather. It nonetheless came to be the base of a large fishing fleet, employing several hundred people, seen at its pinnacle in this picture; the harbour is full of luggers of various sizes and designs. The sloping shed in the background covered a slip where boats were built and repaired.

This card was posted in 1905 and shows a fleet of luggers anchored in the harbour entrance at Porthleven, an arrangement that appears to have been common in calm weather. It enabled the boats to put to sea at low tide. These boats all seem to be of a similar small type, perhaps pilchard drivers dedicated to inshore fishing with drift nets or long lines.

Looking west across the harbour in a card posted in 1945, but it was probably photographed pre-war. There are a number of motorised fishing boats and, against the far quay, an unusual barge-like vessel, apparently handling cargo. The buildings behind it tell of earlier activity: the three-storey warehouse and, at far right, the clay store once supplied by the china clay workings on Tregonning Hill.

Looking out to sea from the inner end of the harbour, with the old steam crane on the east quay and the distinctive Institute tower (often mistaken for a church) in the distance. The Institute was founded by the Bickford-Smith family and opened in 1884. The lack of motorised fishing boats among those in the harbour indicates a fairly early date.

Porthleven

A much later card, posted in 1959, shows the few later-type fishing boats left in the port and features a modern diesel coaster berthed alongside the crane. The port was acquired by Harvey & Co. as long ago as 1855 and coasters continued to bring in coal and supplies for their builders' merchants business until fairly recently. The last coaster probably called in 1964, although the crane had been scrapped in 1959 and Harveys sold the harbour in 1961.

Porthleven is notorious for taking the full impact of south-westerly gales and many photographs are taken of the harbour installations and eastern cliffs under massive attack. This early example by Hawke of Helston shows the outer harbour as a maelstrom of churning water while a wave breaks over the road leading out to the Institute. The baulks which are lowered into the entrance to protect the inner harbour can be seen in place, with the derrick which places them posed above.

A calm day in the outer harbour saw this lovely record made of sailing luggers leaving for the fishing grounds. Two men seem to be sufficient crew.

Looking back at Porthleven from the crumbling cliffs to the east on the track to the Loe Bar. The pier marking the entrance to the harbour can just be discerned while Trewavas Head forms the backdrop.

One of the strangest locations on the Cornish coast is where you can stand on a beach with salt water on one hand and fresh water on the other. This is the Loe Bar (it is sometimes wrongly spelt Looe and is pronounced 'low'). The bar separates the sea from Cornwall's largest freshwater lake, The Loe or Loe Pool. In some way, at some time, the movement of shingle eastwards along Porthleven Beach has blocked the estuary of the River Cober. It is claimed that ships could reach Helston up the river until the twelfth century, but some put the formation of the bar much earlier. The postcard shows the Pool in the foreground with the bar as a line across the background and buildings in Penrose Estate on the right.

Looking down the Loe from below Helston with the River Cober flowing into it. The barrier caused by the bar led to flooding in Helston and it became customary to cut through it, releasing a huge rush of fresh water into the sea. An adit through the cliff at west relieved the problem, but when it got blocked artificial cuts had to be made again in 1979 and 1984 before a permanent relief channel was completed. There is a beautiful walk along the west side of the Loe right down to the bar, the start of which can be seen at right. It runs through the Penrose Estate, now managed by the National Trust.

The coves at Gunwalloe looking west. In the foreground is Church Cove and over the little headland, on which there is a prehistoric fortification, is Dollar Cove, so called after the dollars which washed up there over the years from the wreck of a Spanish galleon on Poldhu Cliffs in 1669. Beyond again are the forbidding Halzephron Cliffs. The remoteness of the church from any congregation is apparent.

A closer view of Church Cove with the church of St Winwallo in its unique position alongside the beach. The Church has a separate, older tower and a main body of two fourteenth-and-fifteenth-century aisles respectively and is well worth a visit.

For a while a ceremony was enacted at Gunwalloe on All Souls' Day to remember those who had lost their lives in the adjoining sea. The party are seen setting off across the beach below the church preparatory, to throw the flowers while some are carrying off the rocks into the sea. As All Souls' Day is 2 November, the weather can rarely have been suitable for such a ceremony and it is clearly rough and blustery in this scene, which probably dates from about 1910.

The aftermath of another rough time at Church Cove; the topsail schooner *Olympe*, 180 tons, lies thrown up on the beach in October 1910. The sea now laps gently ashore but there is a boat and debris scattered on the sand. She had been on a voyage from Lannion to Swansea with pit-wood when caught in a gale. Her crew were saved by a human chain of people from the Poldhu Hotel. (Photo courtesy of Gibsons of Scilly)

6

THE LIZARD: POLDHU TO PORTHOUSTOCK

Looking eastward past Poldhu Cove to Poldhu Point and Hotel and the Marconi masts. In the distance is Predannack Head, partly masked by the lower-lying Mullion Island.

Looking west across the entrance to Polurrian, the four towers of the Marconi Wireless Telegraph Station stand above the cliff at Poldhu. On 12 December 1901 Guglielmo Marconi transmitted the first transatlantic wireless message to St Johns, Newfoundland. He had begun work in 1900 and the four towers followed in 1902. They were used for transmission for twenty years, then for experiments until full closure in 1934. His pioneering work is commemorated in a memorial on the cliff-top.

Some cattle have wandered onto the sheltered beach to join the bathers at the next cove along – Polurrian.

Looking west at Mullion Cove, with the harbour and the Mullion Cove Hotel, another of the large Victorian/Edwardian establishments built around the coast of Meneage.

Mullion harbour is the base for a few inshore fishermen. Here a couple are hard at work off the harbour with their lobster pots while Predannack Head looms behind, a scene that can be replicated all around the Cornish coast.

Mullion Cove looking east on a beautiful summer evening, with the island lying out to sea.

The serpentine cliffs of The Lizard area are at their most spectacular at Kynance Cove, where a number of off-lying rocks add to the drama. Asparagus Rock and Gull Island are the principal ones in this view, which has Lizard Head for a backdrop.

Between Kynance and Lizard Head lies Pentreath Bay ,where on 10 June 1923, the steamer *Nivelle* was driven aground; twenty crew were taken off by the lifeboat but she was later refloated.

LIZARD HEAD, LIGHTHOUSE AND KYNANCE COVE.

Although The Lizard is England's most southerly point, it does not make a clear statement like Land's End. This is because there is about a mile of south-facing coast, all of which can claim the distinction. In this aerial view, looking south-west, the near promontory is The Lizard, with The Point, generally credited as the most southern point, furthest away. Then at centre Polpeor Cove with the old lifeboat station and rocks that seem to project further, and nearest, the cliff supporting the lighthouse with Bumble Rock (not visible) at its base. Housel Bay is to the right and Kynance in the distance. Although an attempt was made to establish a lighthouse in the seventeenth century, the present building originated in 1752. Since then it has witnessed many changes both to the building and the means of providing the light. The original two coal-fired beacons eventually gave way to an electric lamp which is the most powerful in the British Isles.

Opposite: The Lizard was a graveyard for ships, partly because it projects into the sea-lanes at the entrance to the Channel and is surrounded by rocky shoals; partly because of adverse weather (fog causing as much trouble as storm) and also, ironically, because in pre-wireless days ships came close to report to Lloyds' Signal Station, which was on Bass Pont beyond Housel Bay. In this scene the SS *Bardic* is stranded off Polpeor cove while there is great activity around the lifeboat, which perhaps has either been out to the *Bardic* or is preparing to go. The 8000 ton *Bardic* went aground in fog on 30 August 1924 and was refloated on 29 September. She was eventually sunk off the Cape Verde Islands by the German battleship *Scharnhorst*. The first lifeboat was stationed here in 1859 and the slipway ran sideways down the cliff from the building at left. In 1913 a new house and slipway at right angles were built, launching straight into the sea. In the photo, the lifeboat is on the turntable between the two houses. In 1961 the station was moved to the less exposed position at Kilcobben Cove, by which time the Polpeor boats were credited with having saved 562 lives. (Photo courtesy of Gibsons of Scilly)

White Star Liner "Suevic" Wrecked at the Lizard on Sunday March 17th 1907. Photo by A.H.Hawke, Helston.

One notable wreck was the 12,500 ton White Star liner *Seuvic*, which went aground in bad visibility on 17 March 1907. The 456 passengers and crew taken off by four lifeboats were the most people rescued by the RNLI in one go. The ship could not be moved so her bow was blown off and the rear section sailed to Southampton, where a new bow made in Belfast by Harland & Wolff was fitted and the ship was back in service the following January. She was scuttled in Norway in 1942 to escape the Germans.

THE "QUEEN MARY" PASSING THE LIZARD.

In contrast, steaming serenely past and surprisingly close is the *Queen Mary*. The card was posted in August 1936. The liner had been built over several years in the early 1930s and made her maiden voyage in May 1936. It is possible that Mr Hawke took this photo when she was making her first trip from the Clyde, where she was built, to Southampton, hence the close passage. In that very August the QM took the *Blue Riband* for record crossings of the Atlantic at over 30 knots. She had an amazing record as a troop carrier in the Second World War and was retired in 1967, becoming a fixed attraction at Long Beach, California.

As previously mentioned, the eastern extremity of The Lizard headland is marked by the Bumble Rock, seen here on the left. Also visible is the great collapsed cave, making a circular crater in the cliff, called, for no very clear reason, the Lion's Den. It was created by the fall of the cave's roof in 1847.

LIZARD LIFEBOAT STATION, KILCOBBEN COVE

The lifeboat station was moved to this comparatively sheltered position at Kilcobben Cove in 1961, although the sea is probably not often as calm as seen here. The house is reached by a long flight of steps and a funicular lift down the cliff.

Part of The Lizard community is the old settlement of Landewednack, which has an early medieval church and a lane lined with picturesque old cottages leading down to Church Cove. The card shows the track down to the cove with the coast towards Black Head beyond.

Church Cove was a popular destination for the steam pleasure steamers from Falmouth. Here, on a beautifully calm day, one of them, well loaded, arrives off the Cove while interested spectators look on.

Just off Cadgwith is the spot where the beautiful full-rigged ship *Socoa* came to grief while sailing from Stettin to San Francisco with cement to help the rebuilding after an earthquake. In this card, posted in 1907, she looks as if she is still sailing, apart from being awash. In fact she went aground on 31 July 1906 and was refloated when her cargo had been jettisoned. She remained in service for a further twenty-one years. (Photo courtesy of Gibsons of Scilly)

The attractive village of Cadgwith is on an inlet divided in two by this projecting spur called The Todden. The main beach lies to the left.

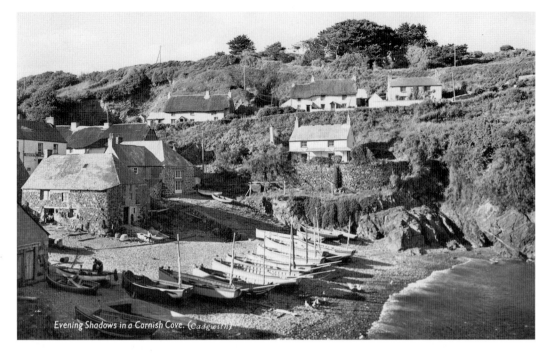

Evening Shadows in a Cornish Cove. *(Cadgwith)*

Cadgwith seen from The Todden with a fine line-up of inshore fishing boats. The card's caption mentions 'evening shadows' but it must be admitted that Cadgwith, being under the eastern edge of Meneage, loses the evening sun early.

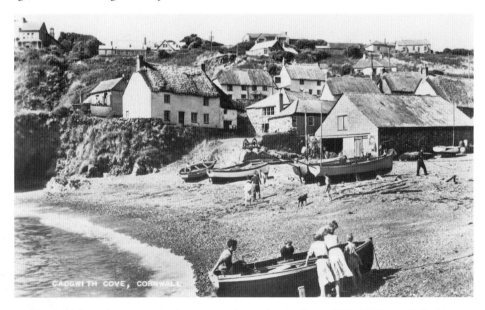

CADGWITH COVE, CORNWALL

Although both cards were probably taken in the early post-Second World War period, this one looking in the opposite direction shows a rather different scene, with few fishing boats (perhaps they were out at sea) and a family of holidaymakers assessing the rowing boat in the foreground. The thatched and other traditional buildings make a picturesque backdrop to both views.

Kennack Sands; General view from South Cliffs.

A couple of miles north of Cadgwith is Kennack Sands, popular with visitors and Helstonians alike. This northward view of the approach shows the beach divided in two by the little rocky outcrop at near high tide.

A much earlier card taken from the other side shows a camping expedition at Kennack, long before the days of inflatable tents. The lady sitting on the wooden footbridge in the foreground is looking at what, rather surprisingly, seems to be a waterlogged rowing boat.

Last of The Lizard wrecks to be portrayed is that of the *Gunvor*, a beautiful Norwegian barque which ran full-sailed into the cliffs at Black Head, south of Coverack, on 6 April 1912 while heading for Falmouth with nitrates from South America. So close in was she that her crew were able to scramble ashore along the bowsprit. She became a total wreck.

Coverack is another ancient fishing port, its tiny harbour protected by a short breakwater from all but strong easterly gales. This card from the 1960s shows a calm summer scene with a group of visitors enjoying the surroundings and a few people on the boats.

The older houses of Coverack on the road leading down to the harbour.

Between Coverack and Helford and north of Manacle Point are the twin villages of Porthoustock and Porthallow ('Proustock' and 'Praala') on their little pebbly coves. Porthoustock had an attractive row of thatched cottages leading down to the shore, but it became known for the large quarries on each side of the cove, from which huge quantities of roadstone were shipped away – one can be seen on the right. The quarries closed in 1958.

Porthallow retained its old world fishing cove atmosphere as seen in this card, with a line of washing as well as the boats on the beach.

7

HELFORD TO PENTEWAN

Falmouth began as a port but after the arrival of the railway in 1863 it began to develop as a resort, with hotels built in a line above the beach. Gyllyngvase is the main beach. This old card shows its western end when little beach tents were a feature.

71

A general view of Falmouth in fairly recent times, looking over the town and the harbour to the ship-repairing quays. The Church of King Charles the Martyr (how many have such a politicised name?) was built between 1662-5, which was about the time Falmouth began to develop as port and a town, outgrowing Penryn further up the harbour.

Opposite above: An early view across the inner arm of the harbour; sailing vessels at anchor, hotels on the seafront and Pendennis Head can be seen on the left. Interestingly there are lines of warships anchored in the bay. In sailing and pre-wireless days hundreds of ships called at Falmouth 'for orders' and from 1688-1850 Falmouth was the base for the famous 'Packets', which carried Government mail all around the Atlantic. My most vivid memory of the harbour is of seeing it thronged with landing craft large and small in the days before the invasion of Normandy in 1944.

Opposite below: Swinging left, a card posted in 1933 shows the whole of Pendennis Head and Castle, a cable-laying vessel and none other than the famous clipper the *Cutty Sark*. She started her career in 1870 on the China tea run, but when that became unprofitable worked in the Australian wool trade 1883-95, making a number of record runs in not much over two months. She was sold to Portuguese owners in 1895 and bought by a local philanthropist Wilfred Dowman in 1922, who restored her and stationed her at Falmouth. In 1938 after his death she was moved to the Thames where she has remained since in preservation, although suffering a disastrous fire recently.

Falmouth, Docks & Harbour.

The Prince of Wales (later King George V) laid the foundation stone of the pier that bears his name in 1903. It is the principal departure point for pleasure cruises up the Fal, to Helford and elsewhere and for the ferries to St Mawes, Flushing and around the harbour. Here, in Edwardian times, four steamers are at the pier, the nearest, *Alexandra*, chock-a-block with passengers.

An unusual scene at Prince of Wales Pier: 'Men of the Mediterranean and Atlantic Fleets embarking.' Huge numbers of men are loading into rowing barges and steam launches. Perhaps they were destined for the ships seen in the bay.

An enormous fleet of sailing schooners, a spritsail barge and other vessels lying off Falmouth. They were probably sheltering from a storm at sea. The roads at Falmouth were always a popular refuge. It is said that in 1815 as many as 350 ships rode out a series of storms. Behind is Carrick Roads, the great expanse of water which runs inland to become the River Fal and its creeks.

A substantial ship repairing yard has been established on the south side of the harbour. In this view from post Second World War days, cargo liners (now an extinct breed) and oil tankers can be seen under repair.

Across the harbour opposite the Pier is the little harbour-side village of Flushing, seen here behind the boats of the Greenbank and Flushing Regatta on 17 September 1910, as the card is helpfully captioned. The competing boats may be Falmouth working boats; oyster dredgers still work under sail in the area.

King Henry VIII ordered the construction of forts to guard each side of the entrance to Carrick Roads on Pendennis and St Mawes Points in around 1540. Both are open to the public and English Heritage considers St Mawes, shown here, to be among the best-preserved of Tudor forts, with its clover leaf shaped bastions around a central tower.

The Percuil River branches off to the east just inside the entrance to the estuary with the village of St Mawes coming immediately on its north bank. It is a favoured south-facing position, making it a popular up-market residential and resort location. In this card there is a trading ketch at the quay (which also dates from Henry VIII's time) and Pendennis Castle can be seen above the steamer in the Roads.

A much earlier view of St Mawes on a card posted in 1904, showing the old houses grouped round the inner side of the harbour.

ST ANTHONY LIGHTHOUSE AT THE ENTRANCE TO FALMOUTH HARBOUR

Left: The entrance to the Falmouth estuary is marked on its eastern side by St Anthony Head, with this rather stylish lighthouse. The huge bell with its striker was for fog warnings but was replaced by a foghorn in 1954. The lighthouse was built by Trinity House in 1835 and was automated in 1987. Behind lie two rather interesting sailing ships, probably a brig and a barque, both with dark and light hulls in the style of old warships.

Below: From Falmouth to Mevagissey there is a long stretch of coast without any major settlements. The first section is the large Gerrans Bay, which towards its eastern end has this fine beach at Pendower with Nare Head marking the end of the bay beyond.

PENDOWER AND NARE BEACHES AND NARE HEAD.

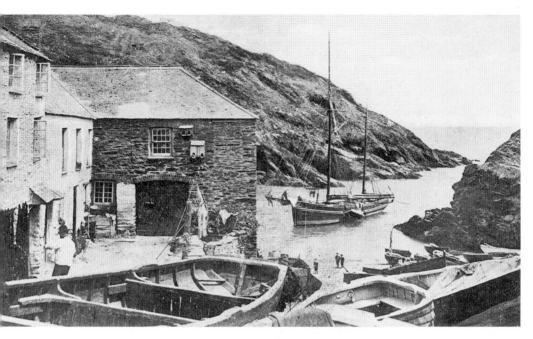

Beyond Nare, the even greater sweep of Veryan Bay includes the tiny cove port of Portloe, charmingly recorded here in a card posted in 1906, with a typical small trading ketch moored in the cove. The ketch has its ship's boat hung overside, perhaps to keep it out of the way of cargo-handling.

Rounding Dodman and Chapel Points, a north-running stretch of coast marks the beginning of Megavissey Bay. There is this small fishing cove at Portmellon, beyond which the near headland conceals Megavissey and in the distance Black Head defines the end of the Bay.

Megavissey, with its narrow streets and attractive harbour, is a quintessential Cornish fishing village, unfortunately nowadays less busy as a fishing port than as a tourist attraction. In this view looking south the outer harbour of the 1860s is seen with a sprinkling of fishing boats and a steam tug which may have been visiting as a pleasure steamer.

In the inner harbour, created between the fifteenth and eighteenth centuries, a great assembly of fishing luggers is gathered. There are also some trading vessels, including what are probably topsail schooners on each side in the background and a small ketch on the right. In the mid-nineteenth century Mevagissey had a thriving pilchard fishery giving employment to over 300 people, but by the time of this picture more general fishing was the norm.

The topsail schooner *Snowflake* of Runcorn moored at the head of Megavisssey harbour. She was well-known as a trader around the coast and in her earlier career regularly sailed as far as Newfoundland, amazing to modern minds in view of her small size. She was thus a fine example of the ships which provided freight transport to the Cornish coast in the days of sail. She ended her days working on the coast of Dalmatia.

Looking towards the village at Mevagissey as it crowds around the harbour. Probably between the wars, the inner harbour contains a good number of fishing boats, although nothing like as many as in earlier days. Nearest is a motorised boat but many of the others seem to be sailing luggers.

A few miles north of Megavissey is Pentewan beach and what remains of the harbour there. The harbour was created in 1826 by Sir Christopher Hawkins, a local adventurer, to serve the mining and china clay industries. The card shows the entrance cut alongside the cliff and the protective breakwater. Despite these works the harbour always had difficulty with silting from the sand swept around the bay.

The harbour at Pentewan lay at the bottom of a valley running down from St Austell, whence a horse-drawn railway was built in 1829. It was converted to 2ft 6ins gauge and steam traction in 1879 and the tracks of this gauge onto the eastern quay can be seen in the card. The quay on the right was served by a trestle onto which wagons were run so that china clay could be tipped direct into ships. The trestle and one of the loading chutes can be seen. The railway closed in 1918 and the harbour became silted and disused. The schooner in the picture may be tipped by low water but more likely is receiving attention to its hull.

8

PORTHPAEN TO TORPOINT

Porthpean

Porthpaen is a little beach only a mile or two from the sizeable inland town of St Austell. It is seen here looking south on a day of long-rolling breakers.

Being so near St Austell, Porthpaen was a popular resort for its inhabitants. This card, looking at it the opposite direction to the last, shows remarkable crowds on the beach and approach roads. There must have been some special event, perhaps a regatta, but that is not recorded. Although the trees are in summer foliage, everyone looks well-dressed, many in the black which was popular around 1910.

Shipping in Charlestown Harbour

In the eighteenth century copper and tin were being mined in the hinterland of St Austell and the extraction of china clay began. There was no satisfactory local port, so in 1791 Charles Rashleigh began to excavate one into the cliff at West Polmear, just east of the town. When it was complete ten years later it was christened Charlestown. In the high days of the sail it was hugely busy, as can be seen in this crowded picture. One wonders how they manoeuvred so many ships in and out.

This gives a clearer view of the little harbour as at a later date there are many fewer ships. Being entered by a lock from the sea it maintained a constant water level, keeping ships afloat regardless of tide. Large horse-drawn china clay wagons can be seen on the central and left quays. The port declined during the First World War and with the coming of larger powered ships and lorries, but it is still there, popular with tourists and the makers of sailing saga films.

Par harbour was also the artificial creation of an entrepreneur, in this case Thomas Treffry, whom we have already met at Newquay. He had interests in copper mines, granite quarries and china clay works in the area inland from St Blazey, which were serviced only by the beach at Par, itself largely the product of waste from the workings. From 1828 he developed the tidal harbour at Par and connected it with his undertakings, first by a canal to Ponts Mill and then by tramways into the hills. The postcard was posted in 1910 but must have been taken much earlier. In the foreground is the main line railway passing from Par to St Austell which still consists of broad gauge style track. The line was converted to standard gauge in 1892and a second track was added in 1893 so the picture can be no later. Beyond it are sidings with clay wagons (which had always been standard gauge) and the harbour full of trading vessels.

A later photo of substantial schooners in Par harbour, with a steam tug in attendance. It was written on 14 April 1916 from the 'Antagonist' at Par: 'We got here last Sunday from Cherbourg. We are now loading a cargo of clay for London. We shall finish loading tomorrow. It his find fair wind for us now and we hope to get away soon.' This is an interesting glimpse of life on ship during the worrying days of the war. Treffry's tramway eventually became the Newquay branch railway, which still serves the great china clay dries at Goonbarrow, and the fine tramway viaduct in the Luxulyan Valley continues to serve as his memorial. The harbour at Par became for a time Cornwall's busiest, but today the deep water port at Fowey is preferred for clay shipments.

A little further around the bay is the small harbour of Polkerris. As the photo shows, it has no natural protection, only an eighteenth-century pier. It had a great pilchard fishery and a lifeboat in the nineteenth century, but now it is quiet.

Around the Gribben Head, the coast soon opens up into the estuary of the River Fowey (pronounced Foy), the next of the great drowned valleys. With its natural advantages, Fowey was a significant port from the fourteenth century, gradually eclipsing Lostwithiel at the head of navigation, as it silted up. This remarkable photo shows Fowey harbour at its twentieth-century busiest. The card was posted in 1932, but, unless the ships were laid up in the depression, it must have been taken some years earlier. If the ships were not laid up, they were awaiting their turn to load china clay up-river. There are three steamers, three large sailing ships in the outer row and four smaller ones, all three-masted, in the nearer.

Looking across at the town of Fowey from Polruan on the east side of the harbour. The town has a number of fine buildings. The tower of the fantastically-named St Fimbarrus, which dates from the fourteenth century, can be seen, with the adjoining Place House, the seat of the Treffry family. Two fine three-masted schooners are at anchor. Fowey was the home of Sir Arthur Quiller-Couch, ('Q') 1863-1944 who, among his accomplishments, wrote a number of popular novels about Fowey in the guise of 'Troy'.

Fowey's seamen served the King in the fourteenth century but became notorious pirates in the fifteenth. Thereafter they served the local industries, but by the late twentieth century only the china clay trade was left. Jetties were built at Carne Point above the town, where large vessels could berth in deep water. In this picture three substantial steamers are loading at the jetties while three or four more await their turn in mid-stream. A group of holidaymakers have rowed up to have a look.

An earlier view of the china clay jetties looking down-river; one can see the railway installations. Barrels of clay are in wagons on the right; two wagon turntables for taking wagons onto the projecting pier can be seen – capstan haulage was probably used. Two fine barquentines are at centre but there is the bow of a steamship on the left. The railway history is complicated. A broad gauge line from Lostwithiel was put out of business by a standard gauge one from St Blazey, then they were joined and operated together and finally the St Blazey line was made into a reserved clay lorry road from Par and all rail traffic now comes via Lostwithiel. Over the years numerous improvements have been made to the facilities, which are now well-fitted to handle all china clay shipments.

Although I have generally not strayed far up the rivers I have included this card to give a flavour of their beautiful upper reaches. Pont Pill branches off the harbour opposite Fowey town and ends at a tiny wharf, where this schooner is resting on the mud at low tide. The main river can be glimpsed in the distance.

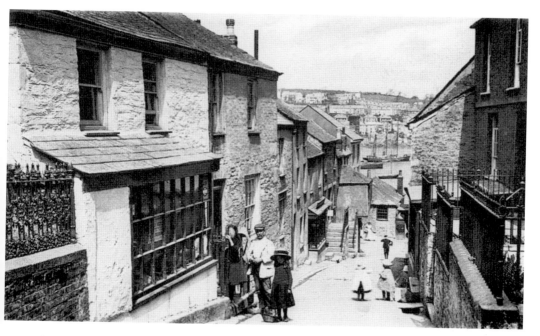

The village of Polruan lies on the headland at the eastern entrance to Fowey harbour. This old card shows the attractive street leading down towards the harbour with Fowey beyond. Daphne du Maurier lived on this side of the river and her most celebrated novel, *Rebecca*, has an imaginary local setting.

Polperro is another classic fishing port a few miles east along the coast, described as 'the paragon of all Cornish fishing villages' and so devoted to tourism that 'every door sports a pisky knocker'. As this old card shows, the harbour is set in a narrow inlet with the village crowded around it in the valley. The medieval pier suffered greatly from storm damage and the present defences were built in the nineteenth century. In this view it is calm enough for the fishing fleet to be moored outside the harbour.

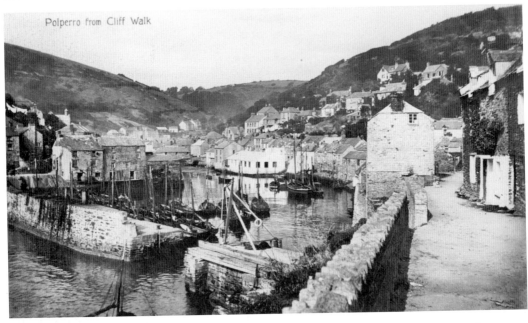

A somewhat closer viewpoint shows the harbour wall with the derrick and baulks for blocking the narrow entrance in storms, like those at Mousehole and Porthleven. The village clusters around the harbour and squeezes into the valley. Today visiting vehicles are banned from the narrow streets and must be parked above the village while sightseers walk down. This pre-First World War scene shows a good number of fishing boats moored in the harbour.

The entrance to Polperro is guarded by this 100ft-high rock called The Peak. It is recounted that during the great storm of 1817 huge waves broke right over it. The pier was badly damaged and many boats sunk. Hard to imagine in this quiet scene with a trading schooner moored to the pier and boats again moored outside.

The Polperro sailing fishing boats were a distinctive type, smaller than those found further west and, as can be seen, usually carrying only one mast. They used a fore-and-aft gaff-rigged sail, which can be seen wrapped around the gaff on most boats here. They also had the transom sterns common on south coast boats. Houses are built right on the harbour-side.

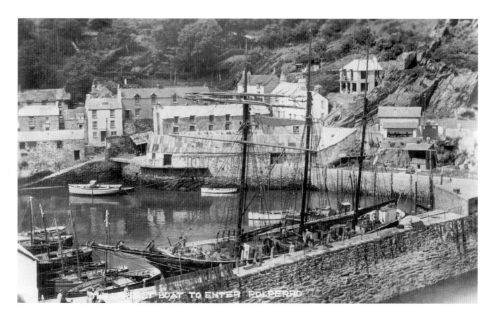

A final look at Polperro shows a remarkable sight. Moored to the pier is 'The largest boat ever to enter Polperro.' Luckily its name can be read, the *Mary Barrow*. She was a three-masted topsail schooner and one of the last motor-less vessels engaged in coastal trade. Built by Lean of Falmouth in 1891 she measured 190 tons and in her early years sailed as far as Newfoundland and South America. She survived a stranding on Porthminster Beach, St Ives in 1908 and was still trading when wrecked on the Isle of Man in 1938. I guess this picture may have been taken quite late in her career, although there are still a few traditional boats in the harbour. It was quite a feat to get so large a ship through the narrow harbour entrance and turned onto and off the pier.

A few miles east along the coast is Looe on another, but smaller, drowned valley, that of the combined East and West Looe Rivers. This view looks out to sea over East Looe, with three large trading ketches exposed by low tide at the quay and the fishing fleet moored in the bay. The pier protecting the entrance, with its circular end, can be seen.

The twin boroughs of East and West Looe were long separated, though joined by a fine bridge from the fifteenth century; they were later united administratively. Looking inland in this inter-war view East Looe is on the right, West on the left, connected now by a bridge built in 1853. Looe had a period of great shipping activity in the fourteenth century but thereafter was quiet, until industrial upsurge in the nineteenth century saw mineral extraction inland which required an outlet. Looe was joined first by a canal and then a railway to Moorswater, whence another railway connected to the mines and granite quarries of the Caradon area. The railway came right onto the quay at East Looe, where a tall derrick and rails can be seen in this card, with a large schooner alongside and a fishing fleet tied up beyond.

A close-up of the fishing fleet at East Looe with the buildings of the West town on the hillside across the harbour. A good collection of more modern boats with engines and wheelhouses, although shaped like the larger local luggers of old and possibly adapted from them. There is still fishing from Looe and it has become well-known for big game or shark fishing.

The coast runs south-east from Looe towards Plymouth Sound, ending with the long Whitsand Bay and Rame Head. There are, again, no major settlements on this stretch, although being so accessible to Plymouth, some of it is, to quote one account, 'dotted with bungalows, shacks and caravans'. Just around the Head is Cawsand Bay, looking out to the Sound. This early card looks north towards Picklecombe Point and shows the attractive village of Cawsand with a small fleet of boats drawn up on the little beach.

Looking the other way at Cawsand on a later date, the beach and boats are again featured, this time with a few holidaymakers, perhaps making a day trip from Plymouth. Tree-covered Rame Head projects beyond.

The eastern end of Cornwall is marked by the great drowned river system comprising the Hamoaze and the Lynher, Tamar and Tavy Rivers, which connect into it. This barrier to communication with Plymouth on the far side was crossed by ancient ferries, one from Cremyll at the narrow entrance to the Hamoaze and another further in from Torpoint to Devonport. The former has always only taken foot passengers; the latter was adapted for vehicles. The first 'floating bridge' designed by J.M. Rendel was built in Devonport and entered service in 1834. In it steam engines turned large wheels which pulled on chains stretched across the bed of the river. The concept worked well and successive 'floating bridges' took on the work. The two seen here at Torpoint on a card posted in 1908 are probably Willoughby's of 1871 in reserve and his later one of 1878 loading.

In 1925/6 the old ferries were replaced by two new ones by Philip & Sons of Dartmouth. With steam machinery set to the side instead of centrally, they were the first specifically built for motor traffic and a car and van can be seen following a horse and cart aboard. The Torpoint Ferry provided the shortest route from much of Cornwall to Plymouth until 1961, when the Saltash road bridge was opened. At about the same time the last of the steam ferries at Torpoint were replaced by diesel-engine ones. The ferry continues busy as ever; it is still the best route between Plymouth and the corner of Cornwall between Lynher River and the sea.

Other titles published by The History Press

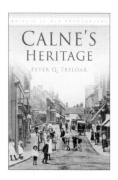

Calne's Heritage
PETER Q. TRELOAR

Calne's Heritage is a fascinating collection of mostly previously unpublished images of this picturesque Wiltshire town. This book explores Calne's history, such as its industrial expansion, the modernisation of the town centre and the community joining together to celebrate landmark occasions. Written by local author Peter Treloar in his eighth book on the town, this latest volume will delight anyone who wishes to discover more about Calne's past and how it has evolved to become the town we recognise today.

978 0 7524 5144 2

A Schoolboy's War in Cornwall
JIM REEVE

Although only children at the time, the Second World War had a permanent effect on the schoolboys who lived through the conflict. In this poignant book, the author shares vivid memories of his evacuation from war-torn London to the comparative safety of Cornwall. Together with rare images and accounts from fellow evacuees who were sent to Cornwall to escape the ravages of war, this book reveals how these experiences are indelibly inscribed on the minds of wartime children

978 0 7254 5540 2

Cornish Folk Tales
MIKE O'CONNOR

The ancient land of Cornwall is steeped in mysterious tradition, proud heritage and age-old folklore. Richly illustrated with hand-drawn images and woodcuts, *Cornish Folk Tales* will appeal to anyone captivated by this beautiful land. Mike O'Connor is a powerful and engaging storyteller who performs at many events across the country. As researcher into Cornish music and folklore, he has been awarded the OBE and made a bard of the Gorsedh of Kernow.

978 0 7524 5066 7

Fishing Boats of Cornwall
MIKE SMYLIE

This book looks at the development of Cornish fishing boats, from the lugger to Pilchard seine-net boats, once as prolific as the luggers and usually built locally. After motorisation, the shape of the boat changed forever and the adaptation of old boats to accommodate engines is examined, as are the famous yards and boatbuilders of Cornwall still operational today.

978 0 7524 4906 7

Visit our website and discover thousands of other History Press books.

www.thehistorypress.co.uk